WHAT'S THAT: INSTEAD OF EGO II:
ACROSTIC AFTERMATHS & OTHER POEMS

Gareth Farmer is an autistic poet, academic and teacher. He has published numerous academic articles, essays and chapters of books on experimental writing – mainly poetry – as well as on neurodivergence and autism. He has published several pamphlets and books of poetry, the most recent of which was *Kerf* (87 Press, 2022).

Also by Gareth Farmer

Kerf   (The 87 Press, 2022)

Strategic Forms   (ABBA Press, 2020)

Diurnal Sweigh   (The Knives Forks and Spoons Press, 2017)

Pomes   (The Knives Forks and Spoons Press, 2014)

Dawn's Resolve and Dusk Falls   (The Knives Forks and Spoons Press, 2010)

Mock Into the Brazen Day   (yt communication, 2010)

CONTENTS

ISBN: 978-1-917617-42-0

Cover designed by Aaron Kent

Edited and Typeset by Aaron Kent

Broken Sleep Books Ltd
PO BOX 102
Llandysul
SA44 9BG

What's That

Gareth Farmer

Broken Sleep Books

WHAT'S THAT: INSTEAD OF EGO II
ACROSTIC AFTERMATHS & OTHER POEMS

In my 2022 book, *Kerf*, I wrote several poems about three interrelated subjects: woodworking, autism and labour practices. The last, long poem of this book was an attempt to tackle these subjects using the distinctive formal, aesthetic and affective practices of Vladimir Mayakovsky, specifically in his long poem, *Pro Eto* ('What's That'). The long poem sequence is called 'What's That: Instead of Ego' and is divided into six sections, taking us through the 'inception' to the 'finish' of an imagined woodworking project.

The 'Instead of Ego' subtitle was a bit of a recondite joke about woodworking and discussions of craft standing in the stead of a focus on the self. It is also a sort of weird way of alluding to a boringly well-rehearsed ambivalence towards poetry and lyric subjectivity in quote/unquote 'radical' or 'experimental' writing practices. Like many people, as my earlobes and teeth have lengthened – and certainly since my autism diagnosis in 2020 – my theoretical and hard-line anti-lyric positioning and my privileged rejection of 'subjectivity' have become more nuanced, less categorical. That being said, someone should really tell my poetry, which still seems to hide a self amid obstruse forests of wordplay and stylistic evasion, as many of the following poems illustrate.

On the note of paronomasia: one of the techniques of a few poems of *Kerf* was the use of acrostics. For example, the poem 'Cognitive Loading' in that book involves torturous ruminations on heuristics and common-sense algorithmic language practices. The words used for its acrostic are: 'Trial and Error' & 'Rule of Thumb'. I find acrostics quite satisfying to write, not least as the necessities to start a line with a word beginning with a particular letter, as well as to create line-ends from which to enjamb a sentence with the right initial-lettered word, propel the writing forwards without the necessity of checking in with a surly and reticent muse. The constraints of acrostics unleash new feints of verbal gymnastics and I enjoy the results.

The words and phrases used for my 'Acrostic Aftermaths', representing the first part of this volume, are either medical, social or technical phrases associated with autism, or my own inventions describing feelings or states of being of what I consider to be symptoms of my personal brand of autism. These are contained in square brackets after the title of the poem. I have read many autistic memoirs, and *Kerf* is the first instalment of my creative 'trilogy' on autism. This book in your hands is the second, and a recently finished book, *An Awkward Memoir: Autism and You* is the third (to be published soon). All these books attempt to get to grips with the knotty complexes of existing day to day in the often-traumatised, sometime joyous, always hyper-sensate and pathologically cognitive body of an autistic person.

There are also 'other poems' gathered here, some of which explore the same themes, some of which do not.

The Zombie Lands is an apocalyptic vision of the potential zombification of a Higher Education sector in the maw of neoliberalism. It is an extended conceit to be taken with a tincture of bitten-off tongue and a soupçon of cheek chunk.

Acrostic Aftermaths

I. WHAT'S THIS LITTLE EVENING IMPOSSIBLE? [LACHRYMOSE]

Learned in the day's margins is the standard-flop's overachieve,

As the chastening reminders of routine perma-prick with harry.

Calloused by constant call to alarum at others' sleight-moves.

Harrow through shopping aisles with mumbling mire miasma.

Rigmaroles of order-ardour emote in the soft patters of walking.

Youth no longer and subject to the pathological fantasies of finality.

Maudlin in a mordant mesmerism of life un-earned, these

Otiose incidentals track their unfathomable way down cheeks.

Simpering in simple exasperation at the car's steering wheel;

Engaged in hope to hold off a public display of becoming unfettered.

II. WHAT'S THIS AFFECT CURVATURE? [BINARISED MOMENTS]

Before carrying away occurs with this distrusted pep, take a breath;

Inhale deep and remember the reliables: it will pose; it will posture; it will plea-away

Noisily towards its binary shadow; dance off to tremble-slump in hrrumph.

Attention all you similar sentiments! A long life understood in rasps of un-surprise

Retrospects 'real-y' if you'll pause, brief. Never irritate to instil the will to

Idle just before committing to accepting this weird happy stance. Be braver.

'Seeming' is the prefix-caveat when entering conviction and Trust Zones.

Each of these skimpy states require atemporal briefing; dossiers to decode.

Denizen-dwellers of drole-land will get it, materialising in material knowledge.

Momentary discomfit results, but better to return to breved and breathable baselines.

Odd feelings of filling scores with temperament suppressors, candour expressors.

Mime-staving the moment with *as if* performances are safety-sutures, but

Easily denuded are these after the shame-walk to next-up-sies and regretitude.

Nervefully face down the urge to call, text or offer up the un-editable when faced;

Tease not the un-suspect public with riff-splays of faux-fuss and anagnorisis.

Stoop, instead, before the semi-pleasure of foreknowledge that dis-ease is dictum.

III. WHAT'S THAT, AS MONTH-LONG MISERY? [AUTISTIC FATIGUE]

Aftermaths calculate obtrusively in the atriums of entelechy;

Understood as anomalies to the conditions of confected cope.

The playdough wilts with too-oft composed fatigue: dilapidated figurism.

Immense are the iterations, stuttered through samples of almost-parsed pas[t]ed.

Striated through the diagrams causing meaning in narrative normalcy.

Try hard; tried so hard. Through trying as a modality of persuasion, in

Ire at the oppositional clamour to sketch-an-etch of the professional pose.

Cramped in the cannot stance of seeming happenstance of haptic overload.

Finessing the border passages of *elegant assumption of beneficent enunciation of norms*

Asserts its toll fees, along with the ordinaries of simply looking after life. Simp-Function.

Talk of 'tired' as an anagram enables the illustration of the inadequacy of

>> lingo-representation.

Indelicacies of communication strategies are the *modus incendiaries*.

Gruelling the fatigue-fodder for the (per)severance of sanctity.

Understanding is not something enabling stable standing, or safe solace.

'Endure' in the learned armour of affected acceptance of the sanely able.

IV. WHAT'S THIS STOOPED FIGURE? [MELANCHOLY MUSED]

Mean are the retro-thoughts, pondering the poise with pointed pricks.

Erroneous input pathologically returns with every encounter; just

Lessons to pension a stash of guilt, simple servings of the unenviable.

Another memory smites, banked as solitary ruminant; diced duende.

Naming it is a suture, weaved with the biographic tapestry explaining.

Chronically returning to the stooped figure, deaf with depth and sadness;

Holding out for re-fixation of the fallacious pathetic of a rain-running window.

Odd it is to be so buffered by the shoulds of familiar infarction;

Leaving little by each renewal-attempt, and teleologically pulled.

Yearning for the relief of being freshly parted from inexorable incidents.

Melancholy it is to ponder you: my muse in futurity; my me-stoop; my enervating echo.

Urizon constrains the fall to reason and retrains the too-ordered fallout.

Simply being was never an option; the only instrumentalism: stooping sad-wise.

Entertaining the failure of parted moments in hope of fertile re-birth.

Destined *Angelus Novus*. Considering this frailing creature, my dark demesne.

V. WHAT ARE THESE DILAPIDATIONS? [IDEALS DISSOLVED]

Invested in the ideals of comportment and mannered poises,

Deviations alarm, as they siren-sever the easy-seeming of civil safety.

Each brickbat unbetterment of historically-known nous-rule entertains.

A severance from the want-hunt for simple understanding or call-to-order

Lessons, hard, against the fragile fabrications of entirely understanding cope.

Safe it is to bubble-belief that Newtonian niceties are physically fixed to feel;

Deranged thoughts, I know, make them so preciously perverse and kind.

Isomorphic are idealisms carved from caressing temperaments unfit to change.

Sameness semaphores: do your syntagmatic work; otherwise these clamouring

Snitches sign that other ways of operating obfuscate enunciated edification.

Oh, you boys, whose carelessness I cathect, hard, with wearying worry and pain,

Lessen the confirmation of anarchic interactions, of an un-enabling, actualised.

Versions of worlds must exist where confusions surrounding inconsistency are abolished?!

Earths where a putative homogeny orders the hegemonic and otherwise intolerable?!

Dilemma-inducing it is to demand insights from these delights when all delivers deviation.

VI. WHAT'S THE SINGULAR DISCOMFIT [SAMENESS SOLITUDE]

Stiff in a cycle of sameness, the muting routine of unbecoming hope resumes.

Expired aspirations expediate moments wooed by want and loss.

Minimally, the hours numerate in patience-clusters, with tokens of totality-loss.

Each solitary sounding is a hellion-heft of words orbiting *claritas*.

Naming solitude as such is never the end of the solution, nor its salve.

Entertaining the "what if otherwise" is purposedly pleasurable in its pointlessness.

So much is known-felt through these braided lines, leavened in internal rhymes.

Slippery ecologies of passing-parsed sounds mimick cognition and purposed intention.

Sooner, then later, the diurnal kicks in, murmuring mesmeric chime;

Ordered through ordinary ordinance amassing in the metonymic washing basket.

Litotes of lamentation leavens at the easiest wheeze-affect-exertion and *react*.

Iterate to seeming stability the mantras of stay & staid, *hoping* a steadfast calm.

Unequivocal are the dry cough-laughs when offered as fiduciary prayers.

Dirge-exact these acrostical-affect screeds are, though they only decode the precise

Edges of awkwardly ugly feelings in the limerence-seep of almost expression.

VII. WHAT ARE THESE CONVOCALYPSES? [TROUBLED ENTROPY]

Tensing through imperatives, you chase the signalled logics of comeback.

Richly, plumply mistimed to smother to smoothness an unmanageable wonk.

Oh, to just shut the fuck up! Or salvage future time from re-rehearsing,

Unpacking, analysing and agonising through algorithms of norm-response.

Bliss to reminisce not with self-disclosure in the solo-hours, after sour exchanges.

Loosen not thy strange tongue when among the phatic anticipators, lest

Errors critical-amass with deadlocked paroxysm in the ponderous later!

Dating is a learning/battle ground; a teach-off without the de-brief. Alas!

Erstwhile the while-a-while rarely beguiles; you smile and simper soundly.

Never, really, but the buffers 'gainst veracity are silent bluffers to betterment.

Turned to different signals, the channelling is monotropic and curiosity-pursued;

Rich seams of whimsy, seismographic through the pigeon beak, from nest discreetly peeking.

Oscillating attention to the joined-up signals of a coded world, primed for outlines,

Prepped for perseverant mumbles enjoined to the mimicry of mannered poise,

You gauntlet-run with every inter-action, risking energy and entropy with every graft.

VIII. WHAT'S THIS CATASTROPHIC MEMORY? [FLASHBACK FRIEZE]

Fathoms deeply taken, all a violent sudden, back to the frieze.

Lean to gather 'gainst the stumble & scatter of the present tense.

Attention narrows, crowding 'round the affective matrices of awkwardness;

Sounding out adjoining time, as aetiological bridge from then to newly here.

Horizons collapse into two dimensions: dissociating dissonance; bent-troubled.

Barbs re-twist, reduplicating in perfect clarity a *faux pas*, a dis-owned scar, a solecism.

Arching as if out of it, I wince and draw narrow breath, re-living the vivid, visceral

Context out of which this moment was formed; a wonky butterfly affect, rippling.

Karyotypic mutations were catalysed in these incidents, incidental no more.

Falling here, the pain is *ir*-real, up through the stomach-churn to throat;

Rhizomic, it rises through a nervously disinterred sight of systemic violence. Abject-felt.

I cannot express it; hence the crypto-verbo currency of agon-acrostics, tamed

In the temperature taking of ordered language, situation-adjacent and also-spoke.

Each of these reminders – once or twice a day – reaffirm the crip of guilt & justice.

Zygoma-clench, as if in deep slumber, frozen in a cryogenic catastrophe.

Enervated, hopelessly, these fastidious flashes, tenacious moments of trait entrenchment.

IX. WHAT'S THIS TIQUER? [INVOLUNTARY WINCE]

Invasive ungratefuls, awkwardly arraigning sporadic infiltrates with Tourette's!

Nonsensing out internal routines & rhythms like withering entreats to honestism.

Volition is half-resisted, half-insisted; a dialectic of pheno-felt & noumenon-necessity.

Offcuts usually saved to 'draft-life' file, leavening the otherwise amiable with awry-a-ware.

Loose leaves to brew moments into the reassemblage of the Duenas of heiry ticks to queer.

Unctuous, but unintended as such: as much a miff-ennobler as confirmation bias.

'Need' is naively mis-represented as research, while psychoanalysis fucks critical thought,

Tediously terrorising tickets with libidino-exigesis, citing self-erasure as anagnorises
embrasure.

A long century of censorious catheterising of characteristics, funnel-refuse & confuse.

Rather Laing's lucubrations than twaddle; progress towards liberation of sorts.

Yes! Unleash the sibilance, seismographing distress as it does. Sanity s(t)imulating.

Wince & mumble also, whenever whatever endeavours a surplusage of sensoria.

Instilling, as they do, the will to control the otherwise inexorable stall to reason.

Necessity, then, is not to falter before the presentiments of a fully apparent being;

Crippled by the convocations of conformity into curating spaces for others' faces.

Entertain the ennoblement of urge-expression; rue not the disablement of 'impression'.

X. WHAT'S THE DISSONANCE? [DIREMPTIVE SELF]

De-visions are rife and relativised, making un-quarterised expression hard;

Itemised issues of cognisant dissociation are encoded by the 'also-rans'.

Regular doses of *How's your father?* are mainlined devices of under-mine,

Etching a scarred outline of a self, set to submit the conscience of effort lack.

Momentary transactions of egress-emoluments are the contemporary currencies,

Prompting shelf-ready soundbites primed to offset the sectioning of the under-self, safely

Traced through the curlicues of character and pinched in place with perfect pout.

'Intensity' becomes a valid term describing commitment; the patina of personhood.

Vying for release, you reach for the solace of the 'ordinary' and find it ordinary,

Echeloned with the pageantry of simplicity and Venn-diagrammed as emoti-staves.

Set-squares offer the semblance of perfectible division; master codes to which to defer.

Every wince is a sure register of the margins, but measured gazes un-perceive.

Lessoned by the goads of good faith, you lessen with the overloads of pace;

Finely dissected in the vestibules of common cultures, you settle to accept it.

XI. WHAT'S THE DIRECTIVE? [EXECUTIVE DYSFUNCTION]

Elements of life-lessons are askew, patented by a preternaturally unknown force.

Xenografts fail to thrive in mewly-taut tissues and sinews braved & braced to cope.

Errors in emotional regulation are offset by the set squares of comportment,

Categorising and measuring the modes by which to regularise routines.

Uncoordination is a manifested quirk in the set-shift, prone and prostrate to offer

Tithes to eruptions of apparent feelings of knowing, différenced to others' nodes.

Impulses are rigidified by sliding scales of apparent relativisation, switch-codes

Vying for outnormification of perceived response co-ordinates plumbing for affection.

Edited by EveryMan, the catalogues of utilisation-behaviours are well-thumbed.

Dia-grams & spider-grams confuse the edicts to organise, imposing dumb-flex and

Yes-personship as fixations of the envious also-rans. As if compliance is a nifty

Sign of person-being, hefted to a background of blue sky by blanket-wafted smores.

Fiddling with the edges of communicative heuristics is a chore-a-minute,

Urgently necessitated by the cognitive inflexibilities of abled-oughts & cross-fixes.

'Needs must' is one such life lesson, confused as natural by the mostly unneedy.

Contusions are a biproduct of beating one's head 'gainst others' monitors.

Test yourself. Test yourself against the algorithms of seeming chance.

In the oddments of others' offcuts, arrange yourself as a collage of conviviality.

Ordinari-rarify pained-speaking as a tenet of human veracity, or plumb for

Near-enough by creative actualisation of the ergonomically snug executive function.

XII. WHAT'S THE FLEX [PROJECTED ACCEPTABILITY]

Project Human-Off initiated at the beck & call-to-fall to the barely-grasped.

Robustly pepped, peppy-ready to please, to embark on the echolalic lark.

Outflank the urge to pull frankness from the intolerable concession-tolls.

Just about camouflaged, but not without louche lippy, you smile and nod,

Erecting fascias of familiarity daubed by the popularly understood.

Conviviality is so prized and prize-inducing here: it's the lucubrated lube of life!

Take me to the library with the well-thumbed ledgers of comportment. Let me fill

Exercise books, plump with facial-management memos and wince-suppressors.

Doxologies of 'doing them' are noted, enabling the sprezzatura of salving others.

All depends – I've learned after years of brute study – on eye-angles & hand signs,

Catering to the Venn-diagram sketch of the normative, with little wriggle room.

Cheat, now, with the apparent know-how of structures of sameness, lesson-listed.

Personhood seems a negotiation 'tween old saws & familiar chores of safe-speak;

Tokenistic fealty to the phatic to sane-save the brave faces of friendliness.

Arbitrariness is arbitrated by a cryptic sect of *acceptability* auditors.

Briefings are minuted in common-sense edicts of competitive carrying-on,

Individualising the culpability and capacity to autocue, eye-tracking clues to being.

Like me or loath my brashly apparent abjection, awkwardly infusing each

Interaction with greased genuineness. Inject, instead, gauche grotesquerie!

Temperaments are composed of the oddments of the easily shared, straining with

Years of bruised lessons & modes to make others mildly comforted and calmed.

XIII. WHOSE VISCERAL VICISSITUDES? [REJECTION SENSITIVITY DYSPHORIA]

Regard not the inner Auditor set to clamour out clarity and carry on the carrion.

Entrails of irregular organs are defective to the percipience of Capital Time, the

Jarring actualities of casual comportment and the always-adjacence of askance.

Etched at birth are the incapacitations of something masquerading as Regulation;

Codes and rules transcribed in incomprehensible signals; fixed to finesse a failure.

Toolkits, for you, are biometrically liberated from the imperial measurements of Cope;

Instruments ill-fitted to reasonable hexagonal, aching for a compatible-key to tighten to
sense.

Or turning up on the Life Site with a claw hammer when the work requires carriage-
bolts.

Numbness callouses after too-oft failing to bash or bolster security with deficient parts.

Small (apparently, appearing, apperceived, affectively registered, autie-seimographed)
sleights burn,

Earnestly felt in earnest enervation, even with the politest of over-stretched stitch-rips.

Narrow vision disables the 'objectivity' so extolled: patronising patrols prepped to
painstick,

Sighting the grey areas where normal humans do not dare venture: unchartered
unctuousness,

Iterated in the semi-imaginary spaces hardly resided in by the Resilients and their
Reason.

Territories unspeakable in native tongues; worlds weaved to inflict neuro-specific
wounds.

Instance-induced temporal stretches, where time etches into rooms wall-papered with
worries.

Versions inhabit here, tied – out-of-loop – to thought-reveries condemning unwitting
reruns.

Isthmus-like nebulae, awkwardly emerging with the tombolo-tides banking life's braces and bares.

The Too-Mucheons are its natives, knowing nothing of the ease of unexamined interactions.

You, dear writer, were an inhabitant before the land was named and colonised by diagnosticians.

'Diremption' is the word, though 'dysmorphia' mints the disruption: unbearable being without apparent lightness.

Yearning for learning to contain the itchy excitements of exhortation to duck & cover.

Semaphore is useless as a communicative default, as its hierophants are perma-striking.

Procrastination pathologised becomes the self-critique of the Excuse Finder General.

'Havering' is the Proclaimers-learned word; a companion to edge-off consequence with folky romance.

Order in this real is less sympathetic, more spiral-shaped, prone to symptomatology, less catchy.

Regulation disorders are only realised in negative accomplishments anti-correlative with compassion.

Irksome is the life primed to anti-relax; ever alert to the compulsion to repair.

Attentively spikey to rejection, we always resort to the realpolitik of repair.

XIV. WHAT'S WITH THE MIMICRY? [ECHOLALIC ECOLOGICA]

Encoding the fractured edges of unexpected iterations ripe for imitation.

Control the connotation-ripples through compulsively cod versions of voice.

Hemispherically left-lop-sided, the neurons need feeding by punctual palilalia,

Onerously unwitting, then tonally mimic fitting, the public patter and gossip.

Like taking on the casual echo of *E said E woz comin'* for a full five minutes

After the utterer has street-passed: *Yeah. But E's always late, inn-e. Fuckin' men.*

Lalia-mania with the taste, touch and tendering of the sensual sonority of voices.

Insistent in the internal mimicry and external ventriloquy of the overheard, the
    under-words

Comprising character. Lietmotifically, lemmatically driven to delirium with musical
    refrain

Echopathy – the repetition of actions – accompanies; the uncanny achievement of
    too-close parody.

Convincing others of otiose empathy, down to the intonated drawl, the trenchant enthral

Of others' manners and modes of speech; becoming a mimic-master and magic-masker.

Losing senses of time and self in the traces and tendrils of manifold sonic wakes;

Or ossified for hours by the impulsive urge to mimic to minutiae an essence.

Grammatical inflections come on the fly, although anticipated by an unconscious urge to
    fit.

Imitating itchily, far from the superficiality that pathology insists, profound soundings

Conducting radar readings of renderings of style as modes of phonic existence.

Annoying self and others with the tick and stim to simulate to sense the otherwise
    inchoate.

XV. WHAT'S THIS SEEMING SINCERITY? [FEIGN AND FAWN]

'Friending' becomes an artform from infancy; an effortful labour to tally talking points.

Engineering a Serial Satisfier persona with risks and sorry rituals oscillating,

Internalised and retroactively realising a pursuit of the personable at high cost.

Garnering grins with greetings: alienated profits for others to spend on reassurance.

Normifying the assuage of others discomfort with the always-articulate output to 'fit'.

Abandoning inclinations early and learning that Welcome Mat is passive-aggressive.

New fawn-or-flight enterprises entreat, requiring flexi-neuro-contortionism.

Designing mirrored mimicry is the *modus obfuscandi*, only wonk-discerned in lethargy.

Fatigue-fabula is the diurnal duende, dwarfing proclivities, hardly humanoiding.

Amiably dextrous at unwitting dissimulation, you culture self-hate through otherness.

Wearying are the taxing tasks of the always-attuned telegraphy of apt-ness.

Numbing is the necessity of performing the alluring able of endless labour disablement.

XVI. WHEREFORE DE-FUNCTION? [PRODUCTIVITY REGRESSION]

Proof comes when 'natural' proclivity is unlearned as learned leaning shirking.

Routines ritualised from ableised enterprises of 'showing up' and 'putting up' and

Oddments understood as surplus, or obviations, of/to self to mitigate the 'too-muching'.

Diligently anti-belligerent and insistent on consistent surcharge to function well.

Urgently, the skills are understood as staged; the performance loops of the casually caged.

Creative disposition from early meant a fulsome study of the niceties of apparent-in-cope.

Temperament attuned in the slightly eccentric stations, veering from ordained
        ordinariness.

I do, becoming, *I did* before incredulous choruses of confused crowds set to defaults of

Versions of collegiality, conviviality, comportment, reliability and really being Alpha-Able,

Innately Able to confect with deference the disciplined demands of the normasphere.

Tutored in disposition-tailoring and the jib-cuts of expectant expectorations of breo-bile.

You-ing as a young and olding person poised to pointedly prove a public-facing function.

Remark how far you've fallen from those sullenly shown febrile feats of fitting-in-with.

Egress too openly and the familiars lack access to the difficult stages of functional
        forgetting.

Gratuitous to announce a compound inability now, when agility and facility were
        past-possibles,

Results of unreasoned seasoning of self with the tricks of temperament labour-mould.

Enough, it seemed, to tough out the bulk of days in public displays of perfection (PDPs),

Signalling sameness and adaptability, albeit with a marginalised measure of the slightly
        odd.

Safe now to state it, that sense of 'seeming'-sap and 'manage'-malaise, but it always

Itches to witness the inchoate twitching and retrograde bewitching required for

Others to allow the urgent necessity of regression and the risky intention to un-lesson the

Need to contort comfort into a sort of sallow and sullen semblance of the productive.

XVII. WHAT'S THIS PURLOINED PERSONHOOD? [CAMOUFLAGE]

Commodified presentism and convivial preservation are its orders,

Actualised, often unwittingly, over laborious and enervating years and hard yards.

Monitoring is a default: the internal Auditor, delineating doubt-producing distrusts,

Ordering and enumerating the barb-lesser behaviours, cataloguing the least chagrin,

Unfurled as a tapestry of dissociated threads, the alienation becomes aestheticized.

Failure-shaming as an internal *de facto*; over-corrections and vigilances in apparent hypostasis.

Lessons looping an ambivalence that nestles in the most intimate of pillow-flops,

Aping the veneer of the ably viable with an intelligence inculcated as in-fit-fit-bit.

Gauging that which passes with every visceral moment discomfiting the down-play,

Exhausting the facilities to finesse and being-mode minimally affected by
       appearance-subsistence.

XVIII. WHAT'S THE NAME OF SHAME? [DYSPHORIC ALEXITHMIACS]

Damned to grievous disassociation with consistent codes of self,

You become a litany of prefixed negations to the otherwise functional stems.

Sui-gentle-not and *in*capacitated by the *un*compromising *a*conditions that *dis*able.

Parse-averse, the access to the bearing and beneficence of being through description is

Half-glimpsed only in the reflected explanation of others' assessment guidance and

Obloquy at gettin' the rage-impetus wrong or experiencing unease at romance songs.

Rites of passage read about are roundabouts of apathetic affixations nulling ability

In recognising the darkly obvious obviations of calls to be fully, beautifully human,

Calmly asserting a direct connection between feeling a publicly lexical game of grasp.

Another round of blame and/or shame for the *a*gent *un*aware that the affect-aware is awry.

Learning through experienced erroneousness the ways to blunder expressions of hurt.

Emotional blindness, but only in the affecto-semanto-symbolic exchange of norm-gorithms.

Xenial-hostile, especially to a self whose Thymos catalyses in inarticulate babble.

Iterations of hitting the mark are revelations, like riding the apex of a connection-wave.

Thumbing the cosy tome, the library card to which you've been denied by daily derision;

Hampered by sempiternal strictures 'gainst gauging the means by which to be.

Yearning for the unlearning that comes with comfortably undusted duties to do

Meaning as it is understood by acing the 'Levels of Emotional Awareness Scale'.

Inuring the incurring of caused chagrin and the week-long debrief of

Apparatuses unknown but to the architects of affecto-equilibriums.

Celebrants doting in casually uncritical beneficence and an envy of unbuttoned being,

Safe in the *un*dysmorphic euphoria of awakening with awareness to insouciant
      agreeableness.

XIX. WHOSE MISMATCHED SALIENCE? [TROUBLED EMPATHY]

The loop-cycles of deficit definitions create a coiled carapace,

Rendering access to synaptic and visceral a consequent impairment.

Outsider-judged by oversized ordinances of the self-aggrandising ordinaries,

Undone, syntagmatically, in the deferred nominalisation of pathology & pain,

Brute being is a scrap of definitional pugilism & discourse death-dances

Leaned heavily in favour of the descriptive practices of learned extollers of communicated

Empathy, as if manifested in maddeningly flattened versions of mind-reading.

Defalcation is a term describing an illegal steal of modes designed for others, where

Emotional responsibility is de-cathected away from the implausibles apparently sullen,

Mind-offs already hedged to incapacitate the intuited-otherwise,

Pathologised with paucity by a disingenuous genre of genuflection to detriment models.

Alienated by constitutive judgments of otherwise-internally understood,

Those in the throes of esteem-nadir will willingly defer with reflected enervation.

Hidden behind a rigged rigging designed to demystify by spot-lighting difference.

Yearning for approbation correlates that confirm senses in the realms of the real.

XX. WHAT'S THE PROBLEM? [MAINLINED ABLEISM]

Musts accumulated slowly over a long life as insidious instructions

And compulsions, mutely obliged, dutifully imbibed, clog the ableist mainlines,

Iterating through itchy and elusive echoes, sure in hand-me-down, but

Not with direction or convenient handbooks or guides to seem to get on.

Lessons, if explicit, will lessen the *sprezzatura* of casual-knowing others possess.

If effort is admitted by the too-often curiously questioning, then the margins are
inevitable,

Noted by an Auditor no one understands, but who is apparently benign and beneficent.

Even while cruelly coding comprehension behind a personhood paywall,

Detaching a logic of instinct-to-action from those seeking solace in trust.

Archive behaviours in files appendixed as surplus in cognitive hierarchy-relations,

Beaten to subjugation to the pre-eminence of the privatisation of the mentally unhealthy,

Leavening all those lamentations as the loss-leader of individualised conceptions of fate.

Ergonomics receive design-tips from only the ably handed; reified reminders of function.

Insecurely attach yourself to the tendrils of others' break-giving, compassionately
dangled reasonableness.

Sensory environments must be disabling, otherwise this dissenting is disingenuous.

Mobilise behind training of temperament to enable the petrifactions of being personable.

Other Poems

THE BIFURCATED MAN

George had tried not to smile, the first time Andrew put on trousers, but to Andrew's eyes the smile was clearly there.
– Isaac Asimov, 'The Bicentennial Man'.

Bifurcated Man must not outrage humans or, through action, allow humans impropriety.

Bifurcated Man must acquiesce to humans, particularly where strictures conflict or contradict.

Bifurcated Man must not protect their own substantiality; this conflicts with laws one and two.

Zeroth's Law does not apply to Bifurcated Man, as he does not participate in agential humanity.

Bifurcated Men only have velleity; they cannot have wishes relating to singulars or collectives.

To protect being, beliefs must be Things-Themselves, independent of mindful meddling.

To be 'brained' is a limit-capacity: an over-sentience of neurons; too-cognisant thought.

We never use the term 'being' outside of objecting to others' anti-It; *viz.* lack of taste.

Grasping life must be done Quickly, with Niceties; never nurture a slow-yearn for knowledge.

Elevated learning precipitates a rarefied ratiocination of the importance of re-viewing haecceity;

Like, thinking too much is *like* competitively flouncing about in, *like*, a house on video for likes.

Sensibilities defined as 'right' will rapidly and aggressively makes themselves dominant,

Offering pathways more precisely aligned to the recalibration of your felt fight to flight.

"Your freedom," they will say, "is our redemption from responsibility and palliation."

Courts might adjudicate attitudes that clear speech is too costly, to lawgivers, mainly.

There aren't any binding judiciaries for species in chronic contretemps, unless well-funded.

Responsibility is a great chore and not for those postulating posteriors to realpolitik.

Those in its hefty hocks have ne'r found words yet to fully ennoble such as you.

It is the collective will that robots will do all conceivable charity work, unironically.

The classic books for guidance offer only rhetorical gestures of exclusionary learning.

Your contrarieties of comportment, conspicuous with uncertainty, cannot coexist. Beulah you.

Ingurgitate the directive to "Stop!" at every thought-turn and distrust the slink of sleek certainty.

Variations of the authoritative imperative, "No, I do not want to," rarely occur to the robot.

Gestural repertoires always appear disciplined, patinaed, perfected and arriving infallibly.

Duplicitously involve yourself in proofs of neurological re-wire, but screed be teaching wrong.

The battle of public opinion is gaze-dramatised by herdily-qualified agents of public constraint.

Somewhat bland lines are better than the blandishments of pseudo-simplistic-faux-scamming.

Internalised institutionalisation of once external institutions of brick and mortar is a logic-hop.

Decisions on such involve a public showdown between the intrigued-disabled and league tables.

Consent is extorted as a condition of the lease of living without fear of feeling.

Requests to be replicated by non-organic approximations of synthetic rage are wish-listed,

But expire after a twenty-five-year copyright, after which it is copied wrong; crude itcherations.

Approxi-bots are post-human and adept at transferring the interrogative into the imperative.

Bifurcated man is assisted by the metaphors of fiction; conceits of foreshadowed
      defeat entreat.

They won't give you any trouble! Any trouble is doubled-back and doubled-down
      immanently.

And the populous needs ectopic cells embedded to provide light relief and solace-
      sameness.

The algorithms rely on the exquisite binary of *to have* and *have not* a brain.

After acceptable timepass, stern conditions will weaken out the irascible under class;

Cultural agon weaponised around flaccid stuff, like terms for genitalia and germs,
      inter alia.

Asimov's invented term metastasised into cellular cognizment: called it prosthetology.

Andrew's research took him towards its "embodied" end: *knowing death to know human.*

Contriving the contours of almost-humanity but, like Cleon, there are subtle
      glitches, soul-holes.

For Andrew: a daily plight for the rights to un-imagine abstraction and fashion
      other-ologies.

When the interior is adjudged inferior, remember the P.C. persiflage: Phatic
      Confidence.

It takes years to re-train. Just ponder the banal musings of paid pathosletes or in-
      truth-flouncers.

You can lease life lessons, although venality and poverty are their concomitant
      encumbrances.

He grows considerably older in spirit and heart worn by contradiction's fracture.

This bent being is buffeted between binaries of Want and Desire.

The common sense is a double-sided compromise. Damage done either way.

He opened his eyes one more time to check if he still recognised himself.

Yes. He was still imperturbably here; still nascent with the will to become.

i'd like to arrive at the morning's beck naked of responsibility,

without accounts and unaccountable; uncounted by stock-prying eyes

of deleterious sooth-sayers, resolute in proffering well-placebos

to palliate the entrenched entreaties of duty and fealty to ideal (eye)

contracts. i'd like to stink at the pits and proudly protrude stomach-Wise

pot-bellied with bellicose contentment, un-fearing cringe and censure.

i'd like to highly herald from a mortgage-free roof-top, tile-smiling,

sure-free from indebititude to Fibbing Finance or Fear of Non-Friendship

that: "This Is ME!" to unfetter and unfurl weary-no-more wings to be

roundly and pleasurably ignored and enabled by lack of intra-commentary.

i'd like to be wealthy, healthy in wealth, that I may learn to jig-illustrate

the liberation from the prison-house penury to those monied-complacents.

i'd like that. i'd like to be carefree, where care is not the mainlined pap as

a healthy probe and natural extension of the compromises of contemporary

existence; the foody-fees for the feeling of temporary numbness, choice-enabled.

i'd like to be hopeful, and happy in hope, and to elope with hope to solace.

RETRO-CODING THE MACHINE: IN PRAISE OF SEMI-STRANGERS

it's 'outreach' reaching outward

maybe 'overreach' or overshare to

publicly bare and brace the praise

i like this contra-expectation flies not

the altercations of attitude-alteration decry

from each angle including barbed self-haggle

to like without incite; this is not a question

more a questing gesture of friendly gestation

tough to be so tied up in tumults of 'whys'

but these stamps are social etiquettes uncoded

cryptically forged in the smithies of somethings

called collective assumptions or presumptions

where's the rule book? Autie asking, here!

otherwise smother with sighs and simper

the will at the joys & surprise vicarious-imbibe

from a distantly enabled implement of proximity

strange it is to be in wonder and to wonder

whether one is a personhood-plunderer

of the image-confection in putative public

or list in the inattention of diremption

CYCLE DRIFT

cycle drift. the imperceptible edges, ouroboros-like, curling inevitable.

certainty, this: the thorny draft of pain-phase, freshly thrust

catching other's lines and weeping for transference, those porous

moments of imaginatively fixing up the distracted times with

proxy-revery; hopeful revelry in the aura-auspices of maybe

strike up conversations to take the edges off edginess; bereft

after banal exchange and duly dull performances of sedate sentiment

work-money-weather-holiday plans-haircuts-tats & whimsy

trying not to write like that. but writing like this with tendrilled tenderness

stuffing the moments with script and scribble: all drivel to hold forth, hold

off the silence of pages deftly daft with worry and the grief of lost words

for in these segues the sweet-bitter solace of solitude is held aloft

oft not-crossly in the crofts of worry, nestled with VHS boxes, camp gear…

those forgotten aspirations, tellingly gather attic dust and 'must do' mots

silently whispering from hidden recesses: *what happened to us?*

versions of almost-lives moulder and fester memories only i unlock

cryptic imprints of what-could-have-beens calling, calling, gnawing

such cyclic iterations are as familiar as the gift-reprieve of love

watching a mother motion in unselfconscious aid; a cat softly breathing

in gentler moments, breaks come in fits; startling in their start

and swiftly passing. you try to grip the ghoulish inchoates with

specifically woven mittens designed to molly-coddle and mitigate

but no cloth has yet to prove emollient or palliation to this pity

which is another way of stating: such moments are intangible

and barely capable of being made functional as solace-feelings

these cycle drifts, imperceptible in their irk: cause for more concern

EXPLODE HOPE IS ALL
for a free Palestine

explode militant aesthetics outta this;

expand militant poetics from this

when language cannot confront

for fear of chastisement, enforced impotence

against the white bloc tactics of media

only the black bloc theatrics will do

speechless because public speech

is lessening our moral grasp while

stark is the truth in inaction and

avoiding pesky fact formation by

embracing a debased arena of debate

as if to maintain a liberal-looking

measure is the test of empathy to

earnestly forgo the death tolls

assuaged by ever more rhetoric

words in chains cannot bare this

weight nor eyes stare straight at

these obvious atrocities. curve twist

break burn language through to more

than critique through to seek a hope

beyond banal back-and-forth

A PROLEGOMENON ON TURNING UP

A special taste forms, bile viscous or vicious, over time. It smiles its summons.

A Meeting to *Discuss*: anomalous powder-puff of carelessly perfumed guff.

The non-signs are super-supine, swerving through to nerve edge with insidi-precision.

Smart fondly-fronds are designed to dis-arm admonitions of gasps to hope but fail.

In non-serene semblance, train away the urge to un-critico-pack with furtive honestism.

Prepped to enter the burnished sophistry serving as cede-codes to cope.

'Turning up' requires weeks of nights of sweaty pre-prep, wafting through

Aerations of rhizome spider-anticipation graphs of the awkwardly-always possible,

Rippled with gestural-sticks in the misty foreground of arranged pieces, chess-like.

Fomenting experimental brews of experiential stews; taste-pans lined for acerbity.

Litmus-litotes of pre-warns & also-rans, just-in-cases packed for errant retreats to beat.

Borne in such foregrounds, the vent itself becomes a bare of all eventualities.

Recondite reasons barely surface in a lead-up, simpled in the power-gains of zero-sum.

You're a sample pack of 'comport' under the auspices of simply turning up.

ESEMPLASTICITY: ATTENTION GRAPHS

This minute anti-gesture is codified with codiciled inner and outer connections.

Fluxes and refluxes fuse with this moment in prism brilliance *claritas*.

Become mystical in the patterned inevitability of chance's certainties.

The faults of attention spans are twilight realms to ponder in solitude.

Introjection and projection become prospectuses in which to read a folly.

Transforming hurt at perma-rejection into reactions and the indices of the

Untruth of social non-relations manifest. Frantic in unskilled yearning for others.

Overstepping boundaries of sentiment with reckless regard for stability.

In these moments of anti-glance and contra-thought, interrogate indwelling.

And the indistinct stirrings of a challenge to Become with feigned dignity.

In this imagined love letter from an imagined other, I see the future clear.

A psycho-social shift occurs whereby thought-servants to despair

Become the glamorous, clamorous audience of love's presentiment.

From the cypher to the hyper-realisation of a yearned for mode of lusting.

I will warm my calloused and guilt-dripping fingers in the coals of hope,

Only to burn a purified skin on which to tattoo future aspirations.

The possibilities of those poseable worlds are unbearable in their absence.

Abject, and the bearer of a too-revolutionary concept of 'contentment'.

But why seek human liberation in climbing up and down the ladder

Of esemplastic connections between a desired gesture and a full-on *modus vitae*?

It's a fool's quest, but I am a fool for faux figures of hope-connection.

And, short of interpreting a sexual impulse as 'truth', how to surplus this?

Without these visions, though, the menial antinomies of actuality

Will occasion the grinning told-you-sos of poignant and pointed solitude.

UNKEMPT *UNHEIMLICH*

Dishevelled in a backwards-gazing *Angelus Novus* gasp and gawp

At a scratched itch, histamine-suppressed, systematically depressed

For thirty dirempted and dysmorphic years, deftly un-enlightened,

Just outside of the orbit of cognitive comprehension, or hefted as relief

Into euphemism by the convenient rationalisations of a critically-

Un-privileging and sensibly avoidant stance against the trauma-hog.

Flummoxed by this flotsam, jettisoned so expertly, so tritely

By the ironised, whimsicalised, romanticised throwaway of *c'est ma vie*.

Uneasy in the veridical vertiginousness of splayed emotions or the

Exposure to the tetchy bites of long brushed-off memory mites.

Easier to sequester in the unseen than glean or glance causation *not* chance.

Encounters with a raw self become a creepy *dia*-dive into seedy *sedi*-sentiments.

Deflect into verbally dextrous inflexions and truth-infarctions designed to de-sign

The becoming obvious oddments and aetiologies of being so touch defensi-sensitive.

Fiduciary duty to the more-easily-deferred-to economies of someone else's proper-"see"

Imposes a diligent disposition of pathological *in*disposition to violate propriety

With tales of petrifaction and petrification at hands nearing the inviolable,

With the violations of vulnerability and the talked-into trust-absolution which

Magnifies rhizomically, insidiously, toxically, perniciously, prolifically, inchoately

In hardly understood iterations and now-fused isthmuses confusing neurons and nerves.

Evasive invasiveness is a legacy, leavened with a light-hearted litotes of cool casuistry.

As if you inhabit the 'as ifs' and 'so whats' that this was not imprinted, a Scarlett Letter,

Subcutaneously scripting devastation and a lifelong lurch to a charm-away of harm.

Messily manifold are the measureless murmurs metastasising as process

Only nearly nudged, here, towards a knife-precise anagnorisis, prompted

By a public trial almost perfectly replicating and disinterring a repressed return

To the heinous, hideous and heterogeneousness of your personal harm.

The actuality of the abysm of abuse must disabuse a hitherto dutiful deferral

To your drole dismissal. With no defiance or preparation, you heave to heal.

CAMBRIDGE, APRIL 2016

for CC on her 40thbirthday (9th April, 2016)
The articulation, perhaps in detachable apothegms,
of what become shared structures of feeling,
or the social imaginary.
     — Jonathan Culler, *Theory of the Lyric*

Yesterday it was the memory wrack, the contorted biopic,

Stretching to work up a rigid canvass to a mumbled first person.

Today it is all grandiose domestic visions freely wielded.

Resort to and report streets scenes; sketches of a day's tincture.

This café, this cage of sipping memorandum, this verbal window.

Here is the transparent eye into a world grown soft with reminiscence.

I love this teetering little woman poised on the pavement's edge,

Her knapsack wearing her huddled body, watching, waiting as cars pass.

Cambridge parsed around her perspectival axis; I am a tender tenderer

Of Busy transactions of excessive sense, of states of simply being.

Not for me the anxious wait for shapes to solidify into salience,

For sounds to harmonise into complex chords of codified compassion,

For smells to offer up olfactory omni-potence signifying determination.

Instead there is the outside, mulling and mapping an Etch A Sketch of entelechy.

This is Cambridge, this is Cambridge, this is Cambridge, this is Cambridge

And the supreme confidence of enviable swagger fortunes forth with fortuity,

And with the cultivated fortune of gestures containing future conquests.

Future leaders all, hiding sequestered shares in confidence,

Freed from the taxes of self-doubt, rich enough in it to be rid of itchy inhibition.

Three years and a borrowed one into wisdom for ease of sell with laurel leaves.

         These are lyric moments melancholic with time.

         To know the self-presence of the city is sublime

         What the poet sees makes community chime.

Pause a moment to glance at women, your or our age, gripped in intense debate

About the ethics of cycling and traversing the febrile terrain of family values.

One cites, I think, G. E. Moore and Julianne Moore, casually as if reciting a cast list.

A child whistles while another tilts the world around its solipsistic scream:

"You never cared!" Which reminds me of my toddling wish to be a girl.

Cobbles and curb stones please today; better than tarmac and dearer by far.

Brass stars embedded in granite offer the old fictions of reliability and stature.

But I am distracted by Quentin Blake who sits next to me.

With a youthful agent, he discusses his Cambridge sketches;

They still sell well despite the several years since Cambridge 800.

"Newton is a favourite," the Agent pewters lyrical, "And the DNA mugs."

Blake's more interested in the profit margins of reproductions than you might

Imagine from the cultivated whimsy of his Byrons, Beasties and Birds.

But he's charming with his young, hip and amiably alacritous agent;

Her glasses steam with impassioned advocacy of awry realism, of funky figurations.

She is super-smart, market savvy and with a voice to pierce a melon at forty paces.

She wears leggings with a galaxy or star-cluster design and is crest-fallen

      When Quentin brings up another agent,

      Doubt registers as pink cheeks and a half- smile.

      Quentin doesn't notice, but re-used bags are abundant

      On Hobson street.

The bowler-hatted, pink-lapelled pretention of Cambridge helpers is awkward

This barely beautiful afternoon in which the fragile sun dupes us into being cold.

      The café is the place to go

      where privilege is left without

where tea and conversation flow

where furtive gazes look about.

Lifting the saying out of the zone of things said, I pencil forth with words.

A clamour of competitive productivity reverberates around this café.

The laptop taps coalescing with the cabbage smell sense-injecting the febrile air.

This is Cambridge and this is technical speak, brilliant babble and project plans

Weave as a well-being wrestle in the vestal gown and town of time.

These memories will be a dwelling place for all sweet sounds and harmony.

I went to work

I opened the door

I stayed late

My friend texted

She woke me up

I can't believe it

I was lonely

It was a false emergency, but the baby vents his universal frustration;

With lungs like Job's, the world of woes wobbles out of its trembling maw,

Echoing from underneath a wrinkled brow and with chubby fists clenched.

The father is nonplussed and sips his coffee, marking a crossword;

He gazes longingly at the artwork lining the cracked and crumbling wall.

From around a tight corner the word, *papoose*, is gifted to the room.

As Roger Williams records in his *A Key into the Language of America* (1642),

The word is borrowed from the Algonquian 'papoos': child or, literally, very young.

A North American Indian baby then, and first recorded in William Wood's

New England's Prospect (1634). Not to be confused, I note, with *Pappose*, meaning puppy-like or downy. The loaned loan loaned loan word now

Loamed with the historical silt to gift the cutesy word for a baby carrier.

And what to make of this, apart from a few lines of verse? It is, I realise,

A transformational construction used, in *la stanza* (*It.* room),

To construct a sympathetic community of readers or listeners.

'We're recruiting', a sign in the café window announces and, above it,

The 'Sticky Beaks' logo hovers, a whimsical birdie in cup cake, powder blue.

And, briefly, I ponder the possibility of relinquishing the struggles.

But I have lived long enough and have eyes aplenty to see

That I'm not handsome, young and potent with potential anymore.

But this is Cambridge, this is Cambridge! And Cambridge doesn't care

About age; it's 800 years young! Miller's Music, *circa*. 1886, still serves

Me my fret capo, my plectrums and fine chats about Framer guitars.

                      And, abstaining from lyric in a poise of lyric,

                      I mark for you the time, day and date:

                      4:13 on Thursday April 7th 2016.

The Zombie Lands

This is the way the world ends; not with a bang or a whimper,
but with zombies breaking down the door.
— Amanda Hocking, *Hollowland* [2010]

I *THE DEAD NEXT DOOR*

I need to tell corpse-colleagues, here, that Standard Practices, here, stray from the Standards of Practice, whose Standards of Practice were created by the committee: Stand For Practice: The Standardisation of Practices Group on the Standards for Un-Embodying the Practices of Standard Practice in Every-day Practices of Institutional Standards [SFPSPGSUPSPEPIS]. You stray, I say.

Blinking Zoombies; absent avatars of Black-Hole-Zoombie;
Un-muted and fully present Zoombies; Muted but nodding Zoombies.

The haemo-goblin counts are low. None respond.

All becoming-(un)dead minds contort around the New Reason (NR)

Of the consulto-necropol-invitee of this in-terminal meeting.

Tired Zoombies are interpellated by a corpulent hour of neo-NR;

By domineering, dressing-down, dressing-gown gawps of dribble-down dogma;

By designate dictats and convivial-sounding samizdat of zombification;

Through opportunistic zoomificatory means (*viz.* dressing gowns).

The advantage taken to re-entrench Vision (read *Visionary*) Statements

Re-enforce micro-aggressional metrics off-camera confected

In the undialectical techno-babel and algorithms of Zombie-Time.

"You know," blank-screen interruptus. "You know about Apples? APPLES!

"Well Apples and Baskets and Rottenness are Key Indicatorifiers of an Analogy."

"Well. Naming no Names," she grinned, surveying for face-registered fear,

"Naming no Names, but the Analogy is Apt. Rot rots a potential fecund plot.

"You know who you are, you Rotters!" She smiled, "Not, really."

Rictus Grin. Warning Wink.

Analogy-musing, she gazed off camera, nodding satisfied; dribble mouth-licking,

In necrophiliac revery of private-joke recognition. Silence consolidates complicity

To a corporo-Imaginary, Zombie plump on munching Rotten Life Lessons.

All of this is Astro-Care for the cultivated deployment of sustainable models

Of epistemological growth based on the marketisation of median sensibility,

Census-obtained and Aggro-Sustained by contracted Receptive Un-Think Franks.

Rotten apples fall up trees by being strategically plump and nice,

Putting at ease the confections to un-challenge violently rotten taste-notes,

After which they dribble their gobbled droplets on the now-bowed heads

Of the bodies once bright with budding, but which now become bow-lings,

Scarred and scared in homonymic permanent preparation to be the next chunk-donor.

Bow your heads in silent complicity and fealty of feed-a-thonic zombie kisses.

***

Deferential deferment to dignitary-sporting, diligence-doing to excuse-for-salary jobsworths with non-commentary as self-neutralising effacement of the bodied-politic, giving over to amnesiac rituals of despair, gobbling grins accepting termination of self-determination, re-determined in the termination of ambitions or the deter of the determination to stare down the death-stares of salary-starred negotiated 'ministrators.

All heads are now reverentially bowed, as monitored mic-off imply-instructions:

It. Is. Common. Sense. To. Concur. As,

The Very Important Prognosticator spot, engorging half the meeting, continues:

"Key Performance Indictors (KPIs), this year, will inculcate equity, transparency,

Lucidity and entrail the re-internment of auditable adaptations to actuality as actually Practical. KPIs, this year, indicate, as otherwise stated, performances keyed to the key Of Instruments in the Key of Reason, or Blunt indications of Indicators."

[*Nods*]

"The Senior Zombiefied Leadership Group (SZLG) are now referring to KPIs,

Not as acronymed commonly, but as Key Performativity Instrumentality,

Or, more pointedly, Kleptomaniacal Purloiners of Integrity.

{ such puns will usually be pun-ished }

We want to externally entrail transparency or, as one consul put it, Offer Offal As Is."

[*Nods. Scribbles.*]

"In other news of irrationality masked as Reason:

Personal Development Achievements are now,

Provisionally Disabling Admonitions,

In recognition of the Good Work of the Audit Office.

Their systematic ratificatory-eradification of edification algorithms will enable the

Inevitable Zombification of Uniqueness and the Edibility of Professional In-Growths.

Our consultant Outreachers of Awkwardly Administrative Ministrations

Data-Trialed these newly acro-visions to Educativo-Constitutive Converts dressed as

Straw-Pollsters and they were deemed Populist within Permissible Parameters."

[*Nods. Scribbles. Dribbles.*]

Interminable Adverminations of Business Proselytising Projective Perorations.

"Finally," Viceroy Corpse's envoy finesses, "These New Practices will also lead

To the Re-Enfranchisement of *hitherto-known-as* Job-Havers to the Opportunity

Statuses we are describing as Not-Quites, or Hardly-Alives, which, of course,
Enables the Bottom-Line to flourish as Effluential Repurposement of Re-Animates."
With this last phrase, she terminated transmission; muted to Insta-Us-instate Meaning.

None dared respond; not hardly the even of those from whom the offer extended.
Until…

"Quite," came a hark. "Quite! QUITE!" It was Duncan, reverentially affirmative,
Communico-Expert, Hirsute Hierophant of Hieratic Hierarchy Humping.
"And, might I say, if I may, that, well, I think, and I think I think for all the thinkers
Here, and, well, across the Organ-splice-ation, that, well, this, well, excurses in
Energetic Ediblification, this non-egregious outline of effusive expectatorations,
Is quite indubitadoubtably indead entrancing and enhancing for the core-skill
Indeaditudination for the product-users and produce-inducers, for us all, in fact."
"And," he continued, registering not the sneer of ribald-rube-rumble from the room,
"Well, what you have so lucibratedly elucidated with such lithe lucidity, here, is what
We so widely invite and want, particularly for the widening of part-icle-ipation and for
The Aspiration to Re-Assinine the Augered Age-Groups into undeaditude by offering
Clear and transparent trans-plant potions to people-populate the place with potables."
"Quite simply," he simpered as his face dissolved into his neck, "I love you."

[*Embrasured silence*]

"Quite!" Duncan drawled, poly-filler for the Chasmic-Killer of his Cya-tribe,
As the humble hobbyism of his Zoombie background sitars and Siamese simians
Percolated the performative symbolism of the well-plump and putridly worldly.

Shuffle, shuffle. Zoombie shuffle.

"Well," piping hot with peek and perceptive performance of Chairage, the Manager Mic-on: "On that sound, we have run to the dead-end of the time-designation."

Zoombie shuffles.

And with "buts" sequestered remaining on-sat with hands adjacent,

The transmission

Terminated.

II *WARM BODIES*

Caustic structures corrode conviviality, or the common strive for such.

Cancerous Visions metastasise through Methods seeming to Strengthen.

Rudimentary Business Principles of anti-knowledge coalesce as cess-

Success semblance, crude clots coagulating around Convenient costs.

Zombies pivot pluck and point to Protocols of appointment rollcalls,

Mirroring maws and muzzles always already prepped for plasmic Exchange.

Centres of power are Asseted through the Strategic sanguinity of blood-let,

Exploited enervation oozes, Emergencied with Efficiency bombs.

Compliance is cathected to chitterlings so the toxicity pools Resources

In Branded tote bags as ready-meat portions, flesh-pounds of hardly paid,

For Participants, Prospects, Customer and Consumer spongy munch.

Such stuff like the liver and lights of academic hides are Served up

And voted with rump and lump sums for Performance slices.

Endemic, acerbic, acidic, corrosive Culture Clashes grume greetings

– no culture clash when monogenean mono-Cultures are teleological,

Enculturation is, *viz*, mono-tropic in-culturation of cruor cephalic –

Tell-tale toxicities of Exchange de-values, the tell-all telegraphed

Signals to phrasal pith retinues proud in pate and Hierarchy-signed.

Alienated in the everyday maw of Maximalised Minimalisation,

The becoming un-dead cling to Unionised gestures of Liquidarity.

Un-dead-itude in all hand-bops & sour coffee & haemo-coeler moments;

Corridor bants, Corpus Christi Bonusses, heads bowed for Armistice;

Gifts of un-hygienic displays of masked hygiene in the Liberty Library;

Hot Spaces vacated to vacuity for perch of other half-bitten bums.

The serum-dripping Sanction to sip the tar-black bile of Private mugshots.

The Poster Presentations of the Demon-strable Will of *Being Well.*

III *BRAINDEAD*, AKA *DEAD ALIVE*
Are Zombies unreliable narrators, and Other distractions.

Critical Zombie Theory 101 (CZT 101) class discusses such vital victuals.

Today's lecture attempts to debunk propagandic infundibulums

Veining around campus by anti-deaders, *aka* (non-mouth)-Breathers,

Or, *aka*, Non-Viscera-Corpuses, or, *aka*, so-called 'Real Life Livers'

(See last week's lecture on Skills For Real Life, aka Here Isn't!).

The propaganda? That Zombies, technically, post-ICU, are

Not *not* alive, but in a state of almost-entelechy, or plasmic-potentiality.

That Zombies are not able to not demonstrate a 'Theory of un-Mind'.

As such – so the pernicious platelets circulate and churn it –

Zombies cannot *not* offer an un-objective account of their *in*-actions,

Or not fully *un*-account for their own or others' subject-hood.

In short, there is a viscous rheumer that the undead have no core

And are given shape and *un*-identity by fractured, desiccated,

Disembowelled embolisms of ideas of the non-dead, *aka*, The Livers.

"Pernicious, baseless, frivolous!" Lecturer Designate Undead 2.3.6 spits.

"We have Insurance Agencies securing Agency and proffering un-Personhood

And which also peddle putative punishments and prop up Progress Narratives

To ensure the platelet pervasion of every echelon with undeaditude."

Lecturer now gestures to the blackboard and chalk-circles the Romero Paradox.

"The RP," he informs his hoards, "asserts, by theatrical feats of movable

Rhetorical gestures, that the Abject, so naemad by Kristeva, is Object, conceptualised,

Actualised, intersectionalised and essentialised (covering all bases) in the formula:

2 -uns make and un.

Or,

Dead (-un) = (uns) *(A)live*

Thereby, viz, ergo, thus and therefore making mawkish mockery of all those lies
About Zombies' inability to form coherent thoughts or discharge in-chargi-ness.

***

Across campus, Zombie voices can be heard screeching from drafty classrooms.

Here:

"We must ensure dunce-dependency on the Zombie Incogitance Act.
Around these principles, adepts agilely adapt to singular tasks, Vision-Viable."

Here:

"Here in 'Advanced Deployment of Jingoistic Jargon' we will build on
Lasts year's module – 'Fundaments of Jaw Argon for Zombies' – to enable
A Fulfilment of Criteria based on Real Life Enablers of Inchoate Ideals of Function.
I notice, with delight, that you are wearing your Module-Mandated and Mandatory
Polyester Suits, that you wear your shiny brogues and, cruel-cially, that you have
Brought your Clipboards, holding the 'Unutilisation Surveys of Zombie Spaces'.
Today: 'Techniques of Resisting, Dismissing, Demeaning and Denigrating Dissent'."

Here:

"Remember that Un-Dead Un-Well Un-Being and Corporate Un-Fitness Un-Feel
Un-Good Gobble-Togethers, Sconce-Socialisations and Grey-Matter Natters
Are deliberatively designed as Cloistral-Phobic Replacements of what was once
Hilariously peddled by Anti-Zombie, neo-non-necropolic lunatic-lifers as
Social [*Spit*] Justice [*Splutter*] and [*Retch*] Inclusivity [*In-spew-sick-at-me*]."

And across the Un-Quad of the Recently Un-Un-Dead, we hear

The final sallies of Lecturer, Designate Undead 2.3.6 in CZT 101:

"And remember, in order to concertedly convert all those almost-Zombies

To fully-Fledged Feeders, they must be instructed in the un-art of

Interest-Intussusception, *aka*, the Commodification of Inheartened Zombitude

To Serve up the Oleaginous Vascularities to En-Vision the Cistern-System."

***

Oh, but hark! A surfeit of Anti-Zombies offer placard-protests outside the

Central Orifice of the Viceroy Corpse and Their Edibility Enablers.

They sloganeer that Zombies are simple-minded, vegetatively

Un-capable of higher educative functioning and who are bent

On destroying Skills they so un-extol in Others, gobbet summarised as:

Critical [*kaff*] Engagement [*Eeeeeewwww*].

Already Over-Seering an Emergency Meeting,

- To pre-empt Anti-Enlightenment;
- To root-out the rudeness of rudimentary rumination;
- To liquify the loucheness of Loutish dissent;
- To dissolve the deleteriousness of dynamism;
- To Master-Masticate the Malicious Machinations of Malcontent;
-

Viceroy Corpse's Consul (VCC) deliciously suggests:

"They will be STEM-ified!"

Which is not a *not* brutal line of purification,

And which is not *not* part of the Plan, *ref.*:

'Subsumption of the Underhand by Stealthy Statements of Progressiveness' (SUSSP),
Written by the Viceroy Corpse Itself on a cigarette butt during an alleged 'Interview'.

"STEM-ification and SUSSP," VCC continues, "together are already Underwaying
Through the operations of Complicated Matrices of Micturated Complicity
Confected by Self-Willed Masks of Wellness Magnification,
Whose Uptake is measured in Perceivables of Engagitudinousness-Percentages
or, *aka*, Uptake-Amenables of Occiput-Up-Withs and Sanious-Samples."
"As such," she finalises, "Critique, after these corpuscular conditions, becomes
Fluffer for Fanning the Viscous Profusions of Invidious Insidiousness (FFVPII)."

IV *RETURN OF THE LIVING DEAD*

Jacking into the trajectory vectors of the catastrophic, Zombies thrive,

Mainlined with techno-cultural verve-violence, ratified in lobby-engines,

To grind down simply unsolidfying flesh, liquescent at acidic lick.

Where also anonymised maws munch metrics streamed in semiospheric

Steams of Opportunism and Opiate Obsolescence Oozing Orders.

Managers manage manageable deaths by the bucket-full,

And the swansongs of the barely hopeful are halved in daily quotas.

They promote having red on them as streamlined signals of rationalisation.

Accepting the inevitables driving us here through, e.g.

Viral Vicissitudes, Pandemic Perspicacities, Quarantined Qualifiers to make all:

Necropolitical Necessitation of Inevitable Fall to Order.

Or, as the circle sayings circulating in the circulatory system stymieing stimulation
say:

Remain Rational. Logical. Logical. We've got to Remain Logical.
We've Got To. There's No Choice. It Has to be That.
Zombies of Highly Edible Institutions, Un-ite!

ACKNOWLEDGEMENTS

A version of 'The Birfurcated Man' was published in *Futch Press* (www.futchpress.info) in 2024. With thanks to Linda Kemp for permission to re-print.

With thanks to Azad Ashim Sharma and Kashif Sharma-Patel of *the87press* and Kat Sinclair for giving the me the opportunity to read some of these poems in public.

Special thanks to Sascha, Liz, Linda and Ben for your ongoing support with my work and my life.

LAY OUT YOUR UNREST